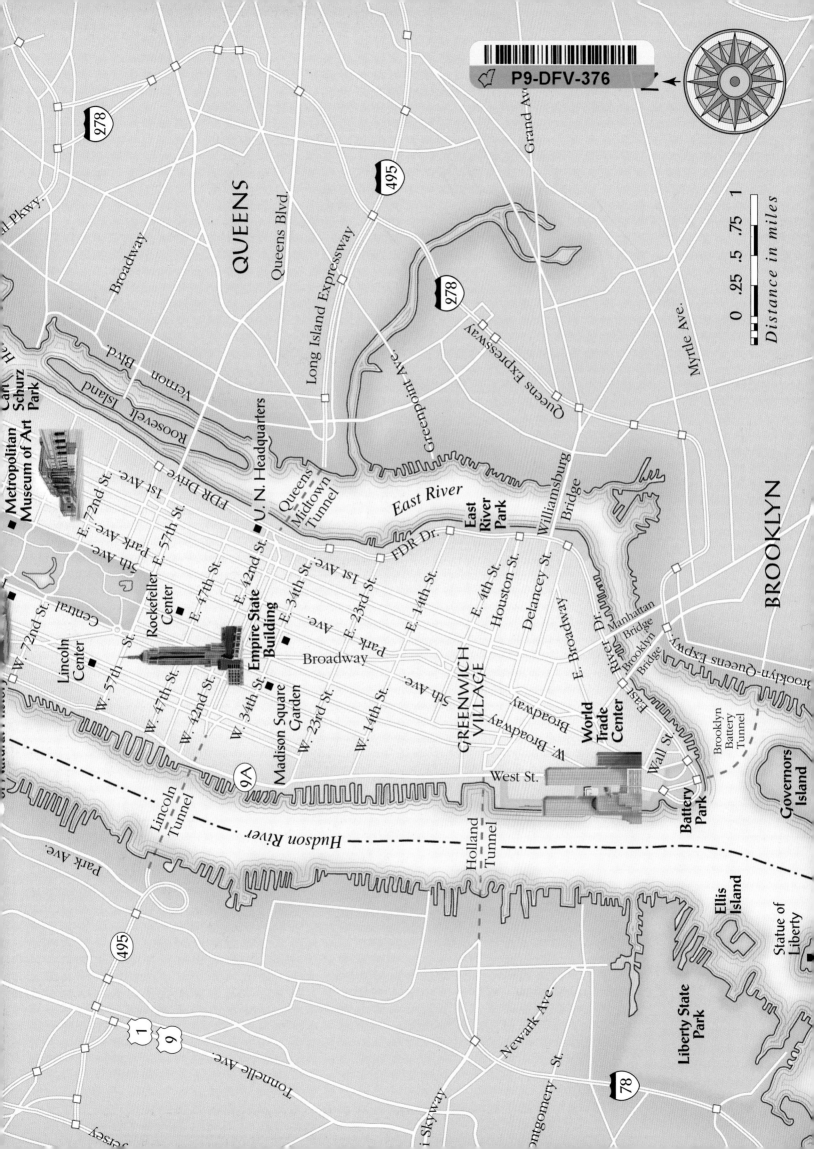

P9-DFV-376

QUEENS

278

495

278

Grand Ave.

Queens Blvd.

Broadway

Long Island Expressway

Greenpoint Ave.

Queens Expressway

Myrtle Ave.

East River

East River Park

Williamsburg Bridge

BROOKLYN

Carl Schurz Park

Metropolitan Museum of Art

Roosevelt Island

Vernon Blvd.

1st Ave.

Park Ave.

5th Ave.

FDR Drive

E. 72nd St.

E. 57th St.

U. N. Headquarters

Queens Midtown Tunnel

FDR Dr.

E. 42nd St.

E. 47th St.

Rockefeller Center

Central Park

W. 72nd St.

Lincoln Center

W. 57th St.

W. 47th St.

W. 42nd St.

9A

Empire State Building

E. 34th St.

1st Ave.

E. 23rd St.

E. 14th St.

E. 4th St.

Houston St.

Delancey St.

Broadway

Park Ave.

Madison Square Garden

W. 34th St.

W. 23rd St.

W. 14th St.

5th Ave.

GREENWICH VILLAGE

E. Broadway

Manhattan Bridge

Brooklyn Bridge

East River Dr.

Lincoln Tunnel

Park Ave.

Hudson River

Holland Tunnel

West St.

W. Broadway

Broadway

World Trade Center

Wall St.

Battery Park

Brooklyn Battery Tunnel

Brooklyn-Queens Expwy.

Governors Island

Ellis Island

Statue of Liberty

Liberty State Park

Newark Ave.

Tonnelle Ave.

Montgomery St.

Jersey Skyway

495

1

9

78

Distance in miles

0 .25 .5 .75 1

Darling Ben (Prom King)
In Honour of your Graduation.
from Rye Country Day School 2003.
our love always
God bless
Mum & Dad
x.

CAROL M. HIGHSMITH AND TED LANDPHAIR

MANHATTAN

A PHOTOGRAPHIC TOUR

CRESCENT BOOKS

NEW YORK

McKim, Mead &
White's 1914 Beaux
Arts Municipal
Building (page 1) in
Lower Manhattan's
Civic Center was one
of the nation's first to
straddle a city street.
It was City Hall in
the days of Mayor
Fiorello La Guardia.
Today it houses a
popular marriage
chapel as well as city
offices. From there
it's an easy ride—
or walk—across the
Brooklyn Bridge.
PAGES 2–3: The
skyline of the West
Side of Midtown
Manhattan forms a
stately backdrop to
drab factory buildings
and oil tanks for those
who drive to the city
from the south via the
New Jersey side of the
Hudson River. Train
travelers, however,
appear in the midst
of "Gotham," with
all of its soaring
towers, as if by magic
after emerging from
Penn Station.

THE AUTHORS GRATEFULLY ACKNOWLEDGE
THE SERVICES, ACCOMMODATIONS, AND SUPPORT PROVIDED BY
HILTON HOTELS CORPORATION
AND
THE NEW YORK HILTON
IN CONNECTION WITH THE COMPLETION OF THIS BOOK.

THE AUTHORS ALSO WISH TO THANK THE MARK HOTEL AND THE
NEW YORK CONVENTION AND VISITORS BUREAU FOR THEIR GENEROUS
ASSISTANCE AND HOSPITALITY DURING THEIR VISITS TO MANHATTAN.

————

This 1997 edition is published by Crescent Books,
a division of Random House Value Publishing, Inc.,
201 East 50th Street, New York, N.Y. 10022.

Crescent Books and colophon are trademarks of
Random House Value Publishing, Inc.

Random House
New York • Toronto • London • Sydney • Auckland
http://www.randomhouse.com/

Printed and bound in China

Library of Congress Cataloging-in-Publication Data
Highsmith, Carol M., 1946–
Manhattan / Carol M. Highsmith and Ted Landphair.
p. cm. — (A photographic tour)
ISBN *0-517-18332-3 (hc: alk. paper)*
1. Manhattan (New York, N.Y.)—Tours. 2. Manhattan (New York, N.Y.)—
Pictorial works. 3. New York (N.Y.)—Tours. 4. New York (N.Y.)—
Pictorial works. I. Landphair, Ted, 1942– . II. Title.
III. Series: Highsmith, Carol M., 1946– Photographic tour.
F128.18.H52 1997   96-44146
917.47´10443—dc20   CIP

8   7   6   5   4   3   2

————

Designed by Robert L. Wiser, Archetype Press, Inc., Washington, D.C.

All photographs by Carol M. Highsmith unless otherwise credited:
map by XNR Productions, page 5; Library of Congress, pages 8–11,
13–15, 18, 20; Bettmann Archive, pages 12, 16–17, 19, 21.

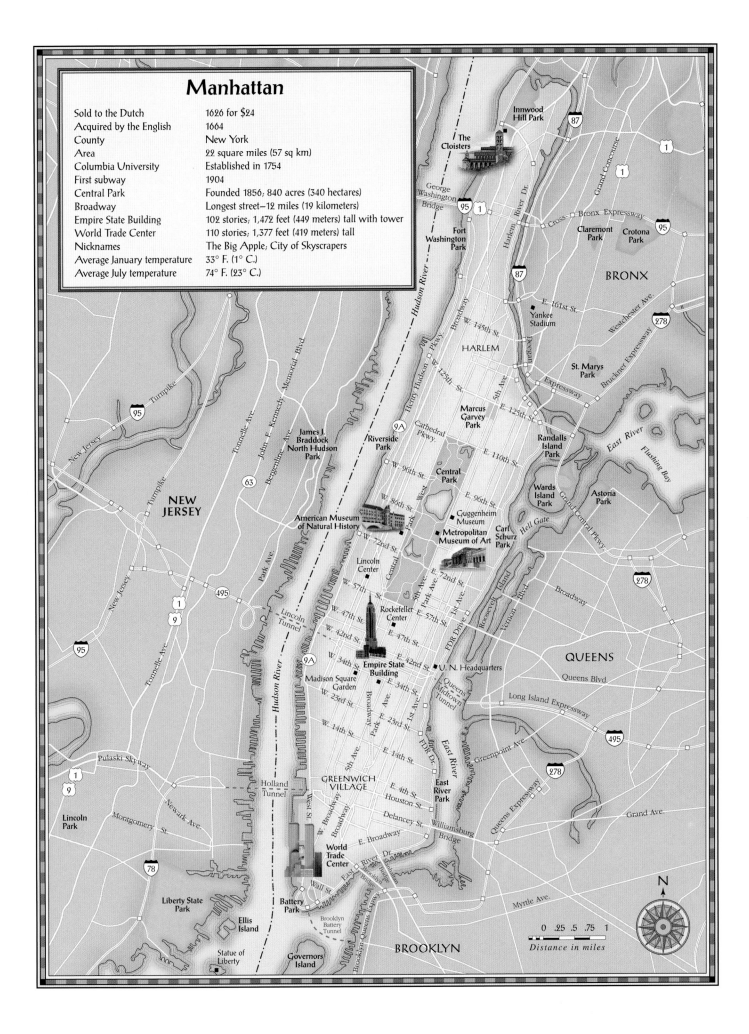

Manhattan

Sold to the Dutch	1626 for $24
Acquired by the English	1664
County	New York
Area	22 square miles (57 sq km)
Columbia University	Established in 1754
First subway	1904
Central Park	Founded 1856; 840 acres (340 hectares)
Broadway	Longest street—12 miles (19 kilometers)
Empire State Building	102 stories; 1,472 feet (449 meters) tall with tower
World Trade Center	110 stories; 1,377 feet (419 meters) tall
Nicknames	The Big Apple; City of Skyscrapers
Average January temperature	33° F. (1° C.)
Average July temperature	74° F. (23° C.)

Innwood Hill Park

The Cloisters

George Washington Bridge

Fort Washington Park

BRONX

Claremont Park

Crotona Park

Grand Concourse

Cross-Bronx Expressway

Yankee Stadium

E. 161st St.

Westchester Ave.

Hudson River

Harlem River Dr.

Broadway

W. 145th St.

HARLEM

Deegan

W. 125th St.

Marcus Garvey Park

5th Ave.

E. 125th St.

Bruckner Expressway

St. Marys Park

Randalls Island Park

East River

Flushing Bay

James J. Braddock North Hudson Park

Riverside Park

9A

Cathedral Pkwy.

W. 96th St.

West

Central Park

E. 110th St.

E. 96th St.

Wards Island Park

Astoria Park

NEW JERSEY

Turnpike

American Museum of Natural History

W. 86th St.

Park

Guggenheim Museum

Metropolitan Museum of Art

Carl Schurz Park

Hell Gate

Grand Central Pkwy.

63

W. 72nd St.

Central

5th Ave.

E. 72nd St.

Park Ave.

1st Ave.

Lincoln Center

Park Ave.

E. 57th St.

Roosevelt Island

Vernon Blvd.

Broadway

278

Park Ave.

495

W. 57th St.

Rockefeller Center

E. 47th St.

Lincoln Tunnel

W. 47th St.

Empire State Building

E. 42nd St.

QUEENS

1

9

W. 42nd St.

9A

W. 34th St.

E. 34th St.

U. N. Headquarters

Queens Midtown Tunnel

Queens Blvd.

95

Madison Square Garden

Broadway

5th Ave.

Park Ave.

E. 23rd St.

1st Ave.

FDR Drive

Long Island Expressway

Hudson River

W. 23rd St.

W. 14th St.

E. 14th St.

East River

495

Pulaski Skyway

278

1

9

Holland Tunnel

GREENWICH VILLAGE

E. 4th St.

Houston St.

East River Park

Greenpoint Ave.

Queens Expressway

Grand Ave.

Lincoln Park

Montgomery St.

Newark Ave.

West St.

W. Broadway

Broadway

Delancey St.

Williamsburg Bridge

78

World Trade Center

E. Broadway

East River Dr.

Liberty State Park

Wall St.

Battery Park

Brooklyn Battery Tunnel

Myrtle Ave.

N

Ellis Island

Brooklyn-Queens Expwy.

BROOKLYN

Statue of Liberty

Governors Island

0 .25 .5 .75 1

Distance in miles

NEW YORK CITY WANTED BADLY TO BE THE CAPITAL of the new United States, and it was just that for five years beginning in January of 1785. George Washington took his first oath of office on the balcony of Federal Hall—the longstanding city hall that had been rebuilt to house the federal government—on April 30, 1789. But when the Congress compromised on Washington, D. C., as a new capital in 1790, then moved to Philadelphia while Washington was made ready, the prosperous city on Manhattan Island set about becoming the capital of the world instead.

Eventually, in order to rival London and Paris and other great cities, New York gobbled up Brooklyn and much of Queens County on Long Island, all of Staten Island, and a foothold on the mainland in the Bronx. The annexation process was completed in 1898 as part of the "Greater New York" initiative of Andrew Haswell Green, the city's former comptroller, who convinced business leaders—and to a lesser degree, a majority of all citizens—in those new "boroughs" that they would get better streets, city services, and representation in Albany as part of a mega-city. The planet's second-largest city (behind London) of 3.4 million people and 320 square miles thus achieved, New York turned its attention to taking on the world in manufacturing, finance, communications, and the arts. The other boroughs contributed workers, shipyards, factories, and cultural attractions, but the heart of New York—and its most powerful economic and architectural explosion—remained Manhattan. To this day, much of the world assumes that this island of skyscrapers, great museums, stores, theaters, and parks—twelve and a half miles long and two and a half miles wide at its widest point—*is* New York City. So do some New Yorkers!

No one can say with certainty where the name "Manhattan" came from. Native Americans from whom the Dutch West India Company's director, Peter Minuit, bought the forested island for sixty guilders' worth of goods (about one thousand dollars at today's value) in 1626 were a subset of the Algonquin tribe whose word for "island," or "island of the hills," sounded like "Manhattan." Or perhaps the name came from the unknown Englishman who sailed up the Hudson River in 1607 and left behind a map that labeled the island "Manahatin."

Almost a century after Giovanni da Verrazzano, an Italian sailing in French employ, discovered New York Bay (but did not stick around), Henry Hudson, an Englishman in the service of Dutch merchants, started off to find a shortcut to the Orient in 1609. His *Half Moon* sailed north and east, around the top of Norway and into the Arctic Ocean. But conditions proved so miserable that Hudson reversed course and headed west instead. Six months after leaving Amsterdam, he was sailing off the coast of Virginia, then turned north and discovered the lower bay leading to what is now the Hudson River. Proceeding up that river, he met and traded with various Indian tribes. When he reached home, his patrons were intrigued: perhaps there were riches and a niche for the Dutch to be had in this land south of French Canada and north of English Virginia. A Dutch sailor, Adriaen Block, retraced Hudson's voyage west, spending a winter on Manhattan Island. Ultimately a new mercantile consortium, the Dutch West India Company, was formed to colonize "New Netherlands" in this intriguing piece of the New World. Small Dutch settlements near present-day Albany and on Nut Island consolidated at the southern tip of Manhattan in 1625. Their leaders built a fort and called the place "New Amsterdam." Ultimately, the colony began to prosper and expand to Long Island (founding *Breuckelen)* and onto the mainland, where a Dane, Jonas Bronck, farmed land that become "The Bronx."

In 1647 Peter Stuyvesant, a stern military man who had lost a leg in a battle on Cucaçao, arrived and took command. By then New Amsterdam was a prosperous place, with busy wharves,

All "eight" wonders of the world—including the Empire State Building (opposite)—are featured in backlit "painted light" glass creations by artist Roy Sparkia and his wife Renée Nemorov in the building's lobby.

Busy New York Harbor gets even more crowded on the Fourth of July or upon the arrival of important personages—in this case, Charles Lindbergh in 1927.

warehouses, taverns, and farms called *bouweries.* The blueblood Stuyvesant was aghast to find people speaking seventeen languages besides Dutch among New Amsterdam's one thousand or so inhabitants. He expelled many of them and made life miserable for the rest—particularly Quakers and other speakers of English, for English settlers were raising his ire by squatting in other reaches of New Netherlands. Stuyvesant was at a severe disadvantage in dealing with the English, however, for his band were merchants and farmers, not fighters. When English Colonel Richard Nicolls arrived off New Amsterdam in 1644 and demanded that Stuyvesant surrender all of New Netherlands—including what is now New Jersey, parts of Connecticut and Delaware, and most of the State of New York—the peg-legged military governor could only sputter and acquiesce without firing a shot. Nicolls immediately raised the Union Jack and changed the name of the colony to "New York" after the Duke of York, who had sent him. Dutch influences would linger, however, notably when novelist Washington Irving's fictitious narrator "Diedrich Knickerbocker" wrote the *History of New-York from the Beginning of the World to the End of the Dutch Dynasty* in the first decade of the nineteenth century. Knickerbocker, originally a derisive term for the first Dutch settlers—it made fun of their baggy knicker pants—came to mean any New Yorker. Later it would become the name of a prominent Manhattan-brewed beer and the city's professional basketball team. Irving, incidentally, also first borrowed the term "Gotham" from an obscure thirteenth-century story about a village and applied it to teeming Manhattan in a series of sarcastic essays.

Where other English colonies had been founded as havens for those seeking religious freedom, and many, like the Puritan Massachusetts Bay Colony, were fairly homogeneous, the Manhattan portion of New York was a polyglot, for-profit venture from the start. Commerce, not idealism, drove the settlers, who even in the earliest days spoke more than a dozen different languages. Little did Nicolls and his men know what a strategic place they had acquired on Manhattan Island. Only later, when exploration moved inland, did the English realize that both Europe and the burgeoning nation's heartland could be reached more easily from there than from any other New World port. With trade came banks, insurance companies, investment houses, wharves, and factories. They all needed people—one day, millions of people—and they required places to live. In two years alone—1847, when the terrible potato famine struck Ireland, and 1848, when revolutions resounded across central Europe—the call for laborers was answered with the arrival of hundreds of thousands of immigrants. By the time Frédéric Bartholdi's 225-ton Statue of Liberty rose to welcome other "huddled masses" in New York Harbor in 1886, Lower Manhattan was a crowded industrial and tenement district. And an even greater surge of humanity would soon follow as millions of Italians and Russian Jews debarked at Ellis Island. These were the times when New York was not the Big Apple, but the "Big Onion," a piquant stew of intrigue, ethnic tension, and clearly defined social layers.

Although apartment buildings would become a Manhattan institution, the idea of sharing an abode came slowly to the island. It was not until 1869 that Rutherford Stuyvesant, a descendant of the Dutch colonial governor, built the first apartment house there. It was a five-story brick structure on East Eighteenth Street in what had once been Stuyvesant family farmland. It featured a common lobby, two wings, and four seven-room apartments on each floor. The building's wrought-iron balconies and mansard roof looked French—Stuyvesant himself called it a "French flat"—for apartment living was well established in Paris and other cities in Europe. Stuyvesant's designer was Richard Morris Hunt, the first American architect to study at the École des Beaux-Arts in Paris. Two years earlier, he had designed a building on New York's Tenth Street specifically as artists' studios, and it would become a model for later sophisticated "studio apartments" throughout town.

Beginning in 1811, city commissioners had laid out the mostly empty upper Manhattan from Fourteenth Street to 155th Street in a logical grid of long north-south avenues and orderly east-west cross streets—all with modest conventional houses in mind. "Stuyvesant's Folly," the Dutchman's neighbors called his new multi-unit building. They equated it to a cheap, vaguely immoral hotel that let out rooms on long-term lease. But all the suites were eagerly rented by young couples, widows, and "bohemians"—including architect Calvert Vaux, who along with Frederick Law Olmsted had just laid out Central Park.

Fancier apartment buildings soon followed on Fifth Avenue, the city's most fashionable boulevard, where promenading in the "Easter Parade" was already in vogue. By 1880, hundreds of French flats, many reconstructed from existing homes or row houses, and most with their own concierges like those in Paris, dotted the landscape. And land was cleared for entire "apartment districts" near Central Park. Most of their buildings "looked like houses, which was an appropriate disguise," wrote Elizabeth Hawes in her epic 1993 study, *New York, New York: How*

The Wall Street section has long been a "dress-up" place, but things were so hectic on the floor of the stock exchange that most men doffed their straw hats and got to work.

the Apartment House Transformed the Life of the City. But not for long. "Housekeeping apartments" like the Bradley Apartment House on Fifty-ninth Street—each rising five, six, or even seven stories in brick structures that looked more like hotels or tasteful factory buildings than private homes—were going up all over town. The true "apartment house" had come to Manhattan. These handsomely appointed buildings were not to be confused with the squalid immigrant tenements that were already a part of the city fabric. "Cheap, hasty, barracks-like constructions without adequate light, air, or sanitation," Hawes described them; "they invited overcrowding, filth, and general misery, and soon became slums." But apartment buildings like Henry Hardenbergh's 1884 Dakota on Seventy-second Street and James Ware's 1885 Osborne on Fifty-seventh Street were veritable palaces, with great iron gates, grand courtyards, hydraulic elevators, and staffs of managers and servants. (The Dakota took its name from its remoteness, as it appeared on what seemed like the Manhattan equivalent of the Great Plains.) Hawes called these sumptuous buildings "private villages." Thus the luxury apartment became a Manhattan fixture, and architects set about making statements in the nuances of buildings all along Central Park on both the Upper East and Upper West sides. Park Avenue, with its parklike mall and set-back gardens north of the giant Grand Central Terminal, also became an oasis of elegant apartments. In 1901, the "New Law" governing apartment buildings allowed owners to take new "fireproof" buildings to ten stories on side streets and twelve stories on major arteries. With that, the "apartmentalization" of Manhattan was beyond control. Fifty-story (and more) apartment towers would follow with the development of skyscrapers.

Nothing could be finer at the turn of the century than a stroll across the Brooklyn Bridge, which Brooklynites regarded as their bridge. It's still a popular pedestrian promenade.

When the Statue of Liberty was dedicated in 1886, its torch, reaching 151 feet into the sky, was taller than any building in Manhattan. There were church spires, some squat brick or masonry factory buildings, four-story walk-up tenement apartments, and—just into the East River off Lower Manhattan—the 271-foot-high western tower of the Brooklyn Bridge, which had opened three years earlier. But in 1887 the face of Manhattan changed forever when architect Bradford Gilbert erected the city's first steel-skeleton skyscraper, the thirteen-story Tower Building on Broadway, on a plot that was barely twenty-one feet wide. The technology had been developed in Chicago, where the ten-story Home Insurance Building shot up in 1885. Other skyscrapers would follow there, but it would be the Manhattan skyline that would be most profoundly changed. Within twenty years no church steeples, no factory buildings, and almost no tenements could be seen in a panoramic view of the city shot from Brooklyn. They were all obscured by soaring office towers. The most sensational were on Broadway: in 1908, Ernest Flagg's 612-foot Singer Tower, like many buildings to follow, instantly became the world's tallest structure, as did Cass Gilbert's fifty-story Woolworth

Central Park's many fountains are a convenient meeting place for families— even those in their "Sunday best"— if only as a place to mop a sweaty brow and get a cool drink.

Building five years later. Dime-store baron Frank W. Woolworth paid $13.5 million *in cash* for his building; for its dedication, President Woodrow Wilson pressed a button at the White House in Washington, and more than eighty thousand Woolworth Building lights flicked on at once. These mammoth buildings, and others like them, prompted the city Housing Commission to pass a "setback law" that forced skyscraper developers to move their buildings back from the street one foot for every four feet that the buildings rose above the "street wall." This was an attempt to preserve light, air circulation, and a vestige of human scale in a city that—more than any other in the world—was fast becoming a series of architectural peaks and canyons.

When F. Scott Fitzgerald first beheld the city in 1919, he remarked that it "had all the iridescence of the beginning of the world." And the most astounding engineering feats were yet to come. Financiers jostled with one another in what seemed like a never-ending race higher into the clouds. Many of these urban beanstalks, like Emory Roth's Ritz Tower on Park Avenue and his Beresford and San Remo on Central Park West, were "residential skyscrapers," with Renaissance, Romanesque, or Art Deco embellishments and surprises like the San Remo's striking twin towers. In 1930, the astounding seventy-seven-story Chrysler Building, with its Art Deco stainless-steel spire, arose. Like so many buildings before it, this was the world's tallest structure—for one year. Then the 102-story Empire State Building became the focus of a million postcards and an architectural metaphor for the mightiest city on earth. It was thought that dirigibles could dock on the building's spire; none ever did, but King Kong plucked Fay Wray from an upper story of a mock-up in the black-and-white movie classic. In the lobby, artists depicted the Seven Wonders of the World and, with some justification, added the Empire State Building as the eighth.

A triumph of Manhattan architecture—and prestige—in 1953 was the completion of the world's diplomatic headquarters, the United Nations. John D. Rockefeller Jr. personally donated $8.5 million to acquire the site, which replaced six blocks of slaughterhouses in the Turtle Bay section on the East River between Forty-second and Forty-eighth streets. Fittingly, the building was designed by an international consortium of architects. Its attractions include the world body's chambers, Marc Chagall's stained-glass windows in the General Assembly lobby, artwork of many nations spread throughout the complex—and outside, the row of staffs supporting flags from member nations. The city pays the police who patrol United Nations headquarters and even underwrites the efforts of social workers who help diplomatic personnel adjust to life in the big city.

In 1961, the city's setback law was modified to permit extra floors above the cityscape, provided the owners would add "public plazas" at street level. This, and the growing fascination with glass as a façade element, led to a further proliferation of tall buildings, many of them undistinguished "boxes" of glass and steel. In the early 1970s the "vertical mass" of the city was interrupted by yet another "world's tallest" structure, the Port of New York Authority's twin 110-story World Trade Center towers. Chicago's Sears Tower would soon wrest the cloud-tickling title from New York for good, but the World Trade Center was impressive enough. Its ten million square feet of office space are seven times that of the Empire State Building. In their 1972 book *The Mid-Atlantic States of America,* Neal R. Peirce and Michael Barone quote Anthony Lewis, then the London bureau chief of the *New York Times,* as remarking when he first beheld the World Trade Center, "It was a sight that cried out: money! power! technology."

It should not have been surprising that Manhattan, founded as a mercantile enterprise, had become what writer Robert Alden called "the cockpit of . . . commercial interchange." Within blocks of Battery Park at the island's southern tip are two powerful stock exchanges, Wall Street brokerage houses, international banks and insurance companies, prestigious law firms, and the headquarters of some of the world's largest retailers and other corporations. Decisions about bond ratings, which can make or break whole cities across America, are made here. The most far-reaching advertising and marketing decisions emanate from here and from offices farther uptown on Madison Avenue. Whole commodity industries, such as coffee and cocoa and cotton, have their world exchanges here. Some of the world's most powerful wholesale firms operate throughout the city's five boroughs, but their nexus is in Manhattan. Retail shopping is an art form, ranging from some of the world's most refined department stores, jewelers, and furriers to the most obscure specialty shops. Name a product, no matter how offbeat—a Peruvian button? a Sri Lankan spice?—and you'll likely find it somewhere in Manhattan. And despite its documented problems with sweatshops, neighborhood litter and crime, and a deteriorating

Almost overnight, the skyline of New York was pierced by skyscrapers that defied the current rules of engineering. The Times Tower at One Times Square rose in 1904.

building stock—some of which it has aggressively addressed with massive cleanup and security campaigns—Manhattan's Garment District, in Midtown straddling Seventh Avenue, remains the nation's fashion pacesetter. Now called the Fashion Center, the district's more than 450 buildings—and its nearly two hundred thousand designers, manufacturers, stylists, models, wholesalers, and retailers—make it New York's largest private employer. Manhattan is also home base to many of the nation's most influential nonprofit corporations, foundations, charities, and philanthropic organizations. And although Ted Turner located his Cable News Network and associated television enterprises in Atlanta, Gannett Publishing started *USA Today* in the Virginia suburbs of Washington, D. C., and the Internet has opened computer dialogue to individuals and companies everywhere, Manhattan remains the communications capital of the world. As the headquarters of network television companies and the home office of two of the world's great newspapers—the *New York Times* and the *Wall Street Journal*—it is the apogee to which all ambitious reporters, editors, and producers aspire.

Chinatown merchants went out of their way to wave the flag— the American flag— prior to a holiday. The district had not yet begun to teem with immigrants and curious tourists.

Great books and magazines, from *Sports Illustrated* to *Fortune* to *Rolling Stone*, are published in Manhattan as well, leaving little doubt that this twenty-two-square-mile island remains the most influential center of American thought. So much so that it took the authors of *The Encyclopedia of New York City,* first published in 1995, about 1.3 million words to tell the city's story.

Manhattan is the crest of the cultural mountain, too. Actors on the legitimate stage can be favorably reviewed and well paid, but they are not true stars until they make it on Broadway's "Great White Way" in the only city with the concentrated population, discriminating tastes honed over many decades, and the money to support three dozen Broadway theaters, Off-Broadway testing grounds, and Off-Off Broadway amateur (and often experimental) houses.

Even New York's subway has been copied. On its opening Sunday in 1904, New York's first 9.1-mile subway line rolled from City Hall near the south end of Manhattan past twenty-eight stations to 145th Street and Broadway; so enthusiastic was Mayor George B. McClellan that he insisted on driving the train for several miles. At first private subway companies, including two that ran trains between New York and Brooklyn, operated independently. In 1932, the city itself got into the subway business with the opening of the Rapid Transit Railroad up Eighth Avenue. In 1940, the city bought out the independent BMT and IRT to become the sole operator of subway and elevated lines in the five boroughs. Manhattan's last "El," along Third Avenue, was torn down in 1955. Trolleys would disappear a year later. The subway's ingenious system of local and "skip-stop" express service, running past the same stations on parallel

Steelworkers pose perilously while assembling a sky-scraper's steel skeleton. It was a sight that would become commonplace throughout the world's burgeoning commercial capital.

trains, would be emulated in many cities. There would be other innovations, such as twenty-four-hour service, the development of tokens in 1953, the air-conditioning of cars in 1967, and the introduction of Braille maps for visually impaired riders in 1993. But perhaps no subway improvement in the nation has had the impact of the Metropolitan Transit Authority's successful five-year campaign to rid its subway fleet of graffiti. Previously, the exteriors of some entire trains had been rolling embarrassments. The cleanup program boosted both employee pride and ridership—and somehow, with the help of stepped-up patrolling, helped to cut crime on the system's twenty-five lines, which today carry more than 3.6 million passengers on a typical weekday.

The trains increased people's mobility and helped trigger waves of ethnic succession, both up the island and into the other boroughs. For example, Hell's Kitchen, long a West Side Irish settlement, is now predominantly Hispanic. The Lower East Side, where half a million Jews once lived, is Chinese and West Indian today. "Little Italy"—once "Little Ireland"—has shrunk as Chinatown expands.

Manhattanites take pride—and pleasure—in the 843-acre Central Park, one of the most important landscaped greenswards ever created. The city had acquired the land—which one report called a "pestilential spot where rank vegetation and miasmic odors taint every breath of air," and on which squatters lived in various grades of shacks and other hovels—in bits and pieces for $5 million in the 1850s. The idea was Mayor Fernando Wood's; he foresaw thousands of jobs for, and votes from, the unemployed resulting from development of the area. The mayor proved right on both counts. Washington Irving and William Cullen Bryant, among others, sat on the committee charged with determining what to do with this wild place. Over twenty years, architect Vaux and landscape architect Olmsted transformed the enormous bog into Manhattan's backyard—a playland of lawns, gardens, ponds, rock outcroppings, paths, castles, skating rinks, small amusement parks, and even a zoo. In 1956, children in Denmark paid for construction of a storytelling center, featuring a life-size bronze statue of Hans Christian Andersen, on the west side of Conservatory Lake in the park. Four roads that connected the city's east and west sides were sunk below Central Park so as to be unobtrusive. With the park's completion, several Vanderbilts and other aristocrats—as well as the *nouveau riche*—began a spate of "can you top this?" construction of fabulous city castles along Fifth Avenue at the park.

If Central Park is Manhattan's favorite attraction, the giant Metropolitan Museum of Art, the largest such institution in the Western Hemisphere, whose main building intrudes into the park between East Eightieth and East Eighty-fourth streets, is arguably its most visited destination. So vast are its holdings covering the history of world art—notably its collection of American paintings and sculpture and its array of treasures from ancient Egypt—that no more than one-third can be displayed at a time. This is partly because "the Met" attracts the world's most prestigious special and traveling exhibits. The building itself is owned and maintained by the city, but its artwork is paid for by endowments, membership fees, and admission

revenue. More defined is the Met's exhibit of Middle Ages art, artifacts, and architecture at one of the most remarkable museums in the world: the Cloisters, a 1938 medieval-style annex high on a hill in Fort Tryon Park in far north Manhattan. Its tapestries, illuminated manuscripts, carved altarpieces, statuary, and even medieval coffins are awe-inspiring; many were the gift of John D. Rockefeller Jr., who even purchased a section of the wooded Palisades below to preserve the view.

The photographers who stopped the action at sixty or seventy stories were intrepid indeed. Even those out west who perched on canyon precipices had terra firma to fall back on.

The Met is the cornerstone of "Museum Mile," a profusion of Upper East Side cultural institutions that include the Frick Collection, which showcases industrialist Henry Clay Frick's European masterpieces in his (since expanded) 1914 Beaux Arts mansion; the Guggenheim modern-art museum, whose spiraling ramps and rotunda, culminating in a ninety-two-foot-high glass dome, were designed by Frank Lloyd Wright; the Museum of the City of New York, which includes dioramas, period rooms, an exhibit on the Port of New York, and a toy gallery; the Jewish Museum, in a 1908 Gothic château that houses exhibits tracing four thousand years of Jewish art and thought; the Whitney Museum of American Art, which *Fodor's* describes as "a minimalist gray granite vault" that grew out of sculptor and collector Gertrude Vanderbilt Whitney's gallery; and the International Center of Photography.

Across Central Park, a smaller but equally prepossessing parade of cultural landmarks includes the American Museum of Natural History (which marked 125 years in 1995) and the attached Hayden Planetarium; the Museum of American Folk Art, which showcases quilts, carvings and other "näive" art"; and Lincoln Center, whose fourteen acres of performance halls, studios, and offices house the Metropolitan and New York City opera companies, the New York Philharmonic, the New York City Ballet and the American Ballet Theatre, the Julliard School of Music, a city library on the arts, and a museum. In the 1950s, several of these organizations had been threatened before they relocated to Lincoln Center. A few blocks to the south, below Central Park and above Times Square, stands Rockefeller Center, a "city within a city" complex of nineteen buildings that displays some of Manhattan's finest outdoor "public art," including the statue *Atlas Supporting the World* before the International Building, and the gold-leaf statue of Prometheus above the Lower Plaza. The plaza is flooded for ice skating from October through April, and it's the site of the city's most famous decorated live Christmas tree come Yuletide. Especially on rainy or snowy days, New Yorkers take advantage of Rockefeller Center's underground passageways, which extend over several blocks. Another favorite piece of Rockefeller Center is the Art Deco Radio City Music Hall, which opened in 1932. Headliners have been as varied as Frank Sinatra, Clint Black, R.E.M., and the public's favorite at Christmas and Eastertime: the high-stepping Rockettes.

Manhattan's cultural opportunities are not confined to a swath around Central Park. As many as two hundred movies a year are filmed in Manhattan. There are dozens of small museums, film societies, conservancies, and arts centers scattered around Manhattan Island. Even Carnegie Hall, the 1891 fixture of New York's Gilded Age, which came close to meeting the wrecker's ball in the 1950s but was saved by music-lovers from across America, has a museum. So does South Street Seaport, the Rouse Corporation's "festival marketplace" along the East River; its programs include a "New York Unearthed" exhibit of artifacts dating to Manhattan's New Amsterdam days. The remarkable library and study of financial baron J. Pierpont Morgan on East Thirty-sixth Street has been preserved as a museum. There's an "Alternative Museum" in the five hundred block of Broadway. In 1995, Manhattan got its first children's museum, located in the restored New Victory Theater on Broadway. There's even a Museum of American Financial History, and a Museum of Radio and Television.

Daniel Burnham's thin wedge of a structure—soon called the Flatiron Building—brought out much of the town to see if the winds it created would knock the thing over.

And the grand New York Public Library, the 1911 flagship of a system of eighty-two branches that was often looked upon as a scholarly research institution, has become a tourist attraction as well. More than one thousand visitors a day come to the building on Fifth Avenue at Forty-second Street, not to peruse its 125 million items—from ancient Chinese scrolls to baseball cards—but to marvel at its architecture, artwork, and the main reading room that is as long as a football field.

New Yorkers and their guests have long made Manhattan's neighborhoods tourist destinations as well. Though Lower Manhattan remains overwhelmingly commercial, a massive landfill project turned its southernmost nub, around Battery Park, from a nighttime ghost town into a "hot" sector of trendy restaurants, posh condominiums, and prestigious yacht basins. Financial towers are bunched together, as are City Hall and other government buildings in the nearby Civic Center; prudently, many law firms established their offices somewhere between these two centers of power.

Residents of SoHo (the area south of Houston Street) and TriBeCa (the triangle below Canal Street) have turned once-grungy tenements

and industrial buildings into cozy lofts, often with eclectic restaurants and unpredictable galleries rivaling those of Greenwich Village at street level. "The Village," originally a tobacco farm that the Dutch called *Bossen Bouwerie*—the farm in the woods—was first densely settled after the American Revolution, when the city's wealthy elite sought refuge from persistent yellow fever epidemics in the tight quarters at the south end of town. Greenwich Village and the East Village across Fifth Avenue remain eclectic districts of tree-lined streets, teeny parks, hole-in-the-wall restaurants, little grocery stores, and even the nation's largest private university—New York University, surrounding Washington Square. Although they are also found elsewhere in Manhattan, clever rooftop gardens and old but functional water towers are found in profusion in the Village. Most of the latter are made of western yellow cedar slats held together by metal bands; water inside the tanks swells the wood into a tight fit.

Greenwich Village has long been a bohemian enclave: everyone from Henry James to Edna St. Vincent Millay to Peter, Paul, and Mary lived or worked there when the living was cheap. Plays and movies such as *My Sister Eileen* glamorized the neighborhood as a place of enlightenment, increasing the fascination with the Village. Several writers' homes along "Genius Row" were demolished to make way for NYU expansion. Offbeat theaters, coffeehouses, and shops have taken over old tenement buildings in the grimy East Village. But rising housing prices and the influx of gawking tourists have prompted many writers and artists to move elsewhere. "The Bowery"—which began as another Dutch farm on the island's Lower East Side—was the home of a succession of immigrant groups, notably, in recent years, Chinese spilling over from Chinatown. The Bowery was also the name given to an early post road up to Harlem and thence

Lower Broadway, looking north from Bowling Green, was known as New York's "Grand Canyon." The street is associated with the Theater District, but it runs almost the length of Manhattan.

out of the city to Albany and Boston; a smidgen of it remains as a crowded Lower Manhattan avenue today. All of these communities, as well as Chinatown and Little Italy, lie below Fourteenth Street, meaning they developed higgledy-piggledy before the city's orderly grid plan was developed. Street names disappear, then reappear; roads curve and twist and intersect in improbable places; avenues run parallel to streets in spots; and most all the streets are narrow and crowded to boot.

Above Fourteenth Street, Chelsea has preserved townhouses and writers' garrets. The neighborhood was named by Captain Thomas Clarke, who built an estate in the area in 1750, after the site of the famous soldier's home in London. The area was later subdivided by Clarke's grandson, Clement Clarke Moore, who became far more famous as the author of the poem "The Night Before Christmas." Murray Hill, Gramercy Park, and Madison Square in Midtown were, in turn, Manhattan's most opulent residential addresses early in the century, and the leafy charm of their brownstone mansions and townhouses endures. Forty-second Street, an increasingly less seedy but still-colorful crosstown thoroughfare, connects the United Nations on the east to the Grand Central Terminal—the city's renovated Beaux Arts commuter nerve center—and to Times Square, the "Crossroads of the World." The square is of course triangular, as everyone knows who has photographed its pulsating neon billboards or counted down the Old Year as a two-hundred-pound lighted ball slides down a flagpole there. Some of Times Square's sixty jumbo signs are half a block long; the famous four-story Coca-Cola bottle that fills and refills itself contains a mile of neon tubing and thirteen thousand light bulbs. Once "dead, desolate, dismal, and dreary,"

Florenz Ziegfeld produced his Follies *revue at the New Amsterdam Theater on West Forty-second Street. The Art Nouveau theater later fell on hard times and became a "B-picture" movie house.*

in the words of Nan Robertson, head of an ambitious Forty-second Street Development Project, Times Square is enjoying a glittering renewal, as the Disney Company and other corporations refurbish and even move theaters and replace adult bookstores and peep shows with movie complexes and a tourist hotel. The *New York Times* newspaper itself long ago moved a block away to Forty-third Street, but Times Square remains the gateway to "Broadway."

Broadway—the street—angles west of Central Park through the Upper West Side, where previously disreputable avenues like Columbus and Amsterdam have also been revived by clusters of boutiques and bodegas. Walls of co-op brownstone apartment buildings along Riverside Drive, West End Avenue, and Central Park West—and more modest townhouses along side streets—have been re-gentrified and, while not yet as stylish as their counterparts on the silk-stocking Upper East Side, are the rage.

The Upper East Side had long been a favorite address of New York's business and social elite. American Fur Company tycoon John Jacob Astor built a country estate overlooking the East River there around 1800. So did prosperous Knickerbockers and a Scotsman named Archibald Gracie, whose mansion in Carl Schurz Park—the only Upper East Side homestead from the period still standing—is now the residence of New York City's mayor. Further development was spurred by the construction of elevated transit lines along Second and Third avenues in the 1880s. Blocks of brownstones and tenement apartment buildings crowded out breweries and factories. Not just industrial titans moved in; so did working-class Germans, Hungarians, Irish, and Czechs who were abandoning the deteriorating Lower East Side. A spurt of building—and the eviction of many tenants of modest means—followed. It was fueled by developers' desire to get luxury elevator apartments in the ground before a more restrictive zoning code, set for 1961, could take effect. While many elderly residents hung on to their Upper East Side apartments, much of the colorful immigrant character of the neighborhood has disappeared.

Fodor's describes the high ridge north and west of Central Park as a cultural outpost: "Columbia University, which developed the mind; Saint Luke's Hospital, which cared for the body; and the Cathedral of Saint John the Divine, which tended the soul." That ornate, Gothic Episcopal cathedral on Columbus Avenue, which has been in seemingly perpetual construction and renovation since the cornerstone was first laid in 1892, will be the world's largest cathedral once the work is completed. It, the Moorish-style Central Synagogue on Lexington Avenue; Saint Patrick's Catholic cathedral on Fifth Avenue; and Harlem's Abyssinian Baptist Church, the home church of both Adam Clayton Powell Sr. and Adam Clayton Powell Jr. on West 138th Street in Harlem, are among the most visited and photographed buildings in Manhattan. As a testament to the city's ever-evolving ethnic mix, it's not unusual to find churches located in former synagogues, and vice versa, mosques in old church buildings, and words carved into the stone and stained-glass windows of houses of worship in languages that are no longer spoken inside.

Harlem was settled by Dutch farmers, who named it *Nieuw Haarlem* for the city of Haarlem in Holland. The English later shortened the name. James Roosevelt, the great-grandfather of Franklin D. Roosevelt, was among Harlem's farmers. The New York and Harlem Railroad (originally a horse-car line) reached the area in 1837, spurring migration. When the subway

The imposing main hall of the 1910 Penn Station was dominated by arched steel and glass windows. Despite picketing by architects, the station was demolished in 1962.

When it was first completed in the heart of the Great Depression, the Empire State Building had such difficulty renting offices that it was mockingly called the "Empty State Building."

arrived at the beginning of the twentieth century, developers earmarked Harlem as a suburb, and thousands of Germans, Jews, and Italians moved in. But after World War I, the families of returning servicemen began to move to newer housing in the Bronx and the suburbs. As African Americans moved in, Harlem became the intellectual, cultural, and symbolic capital of Black America. In the new black neighborhood, nightclubs and jazz joints jumped (with a white clientele) in the Roaring Twenties, and African Americans settled into pleasant row houses and brownstones. Many later departed for the true suburbs, however, and unemployment ravaged the area in the Great Depression. Left behind in many parts of Harlem was a slum whose misery was compounded when the city located, and then neglected, huge, overcrowded public-housing projects there. Residents of Harlem and the adjacent "Spanish Harlem" have made significant strides in rebuilding their communities. Attractions such as the refurbished Apollo Theater and the Studio Museum, both on Martin Luther King Jr. Boulevard (formerly West 125th Street), have energized the neighborhood, as has the ripple of renovations of many old homes.

Alexander Hamilton once owned a country home in Washington Heights, the narrow northern tip of the island above Harlem. The area had been a common ground for landowners in *Nieuw Haarlem*. Eventually it was renamed for George Washington, who headquartered in the Jumel Mansion there briefly during the American Revolution before British and Hessian forces took Forts Washington and George and forced the Americans out. The Crown would hold Manhattan throughout the remainder of the war; afterward, when British soldiers marched to their ships for the ignominious sail home, Manhattanites accorded them a respectful farewell. Today the island's northern reaches are a mélange of poor and middle-income neighborhoods, hilly parks and ridges, Yeshiva University's main campus, and a ribbon of roads leading to the eastern terminus of the George Washington Bridge.

In the midst of Manhattan's residential neighborhoods and office towers are some of the most luxurious (and also some modest but comfortable) hotels in the nation, so many thousands of restaurants that the city lost count somewhere past ten thousand, incalculable numbers of specialty shops and museums, bookstores and flea markets of every description, and the Madison Square Garden complex that is home to Rangers hockey, Knicks basketball, and numerous prizefights and other special events. Manhattan lost its pro football team to the Bronx when the New York Giants moved to Yankee Stadium in 1955, and major league baseball when the team of the same name bolted for San Francisco in 1958. Some might claim that neither had been treasured with the kind of home-town zeal that Brooklyn showered on its Dodgers, or the Bronx regards its Yankees.

Getting around town is often a challenge and occasionally an adventure. Manhattan at times seems like an undulating yellow beehive of honking taxicabs. Driving and parking one's personal automobile are time-consuming, expensive, and often frustrating experiences. As a result, many Manhattanites own no car at all, and the efficient subways are patronized by seven-figure Wall Street executives, middle-income civil servants, out-of-work writers and actors, homeless street people, and fascinated tourists alike. And New Yorkers are always being watched!

Thousands of sightseers in tour buses, limousines, helicopters, and cruise ships gape at the passing throngs as well as buildings; there are even cruises on the Hudson exclusively in languages besides English—including Portuguese, Spanish, Italian, Japanese, French, and German.

Police officers were kept busy making the city safer in the 1990s. The police commissioner's crackdown on "quality of life" offenses such as aggressive panhandling noticeably improved the tenor of the town. In places like Bryant Park, where drugs were once openly dealt, picnicking, public concerts, and even outdoor movies brought civilization back with a flourish.

Except in a few sanctums of relaxation like Central Park or a coffeehouse, the city is an urban dervish in perpetual motion, forever on deadline. Manhattan truly does not sleep, as anyone who has walked the streets or peered out a hotel window at three in the morning can attest. Rather, it just lowers the din. Many New Yorkers have acclimated to the frenzy. They walk faster, sometimes talk faster, and—in order to succeed in the toughest town in the land—occasionally think faster than others as well. There's never a lack of something to do, someplace to go, someone to see on this island of 1.5 million residents, a million more workers, and half a million weekly visitors. Manhattan, purchased for those sixty guilders of trinkets almost four centuries ago, is today a world capital of not only finance, culture, diplomacy, and communications, but of sheer excitement as well.

The lights of a Manhattan evening (below) have long inspired awe. The island's electric bill is even more astronomical today (overleaf). The outlined silhouette at the center is South Street Seaport. Beneath the city's six thousand miles of streets run sixty-two thousand miles of electrical wires and conduits.

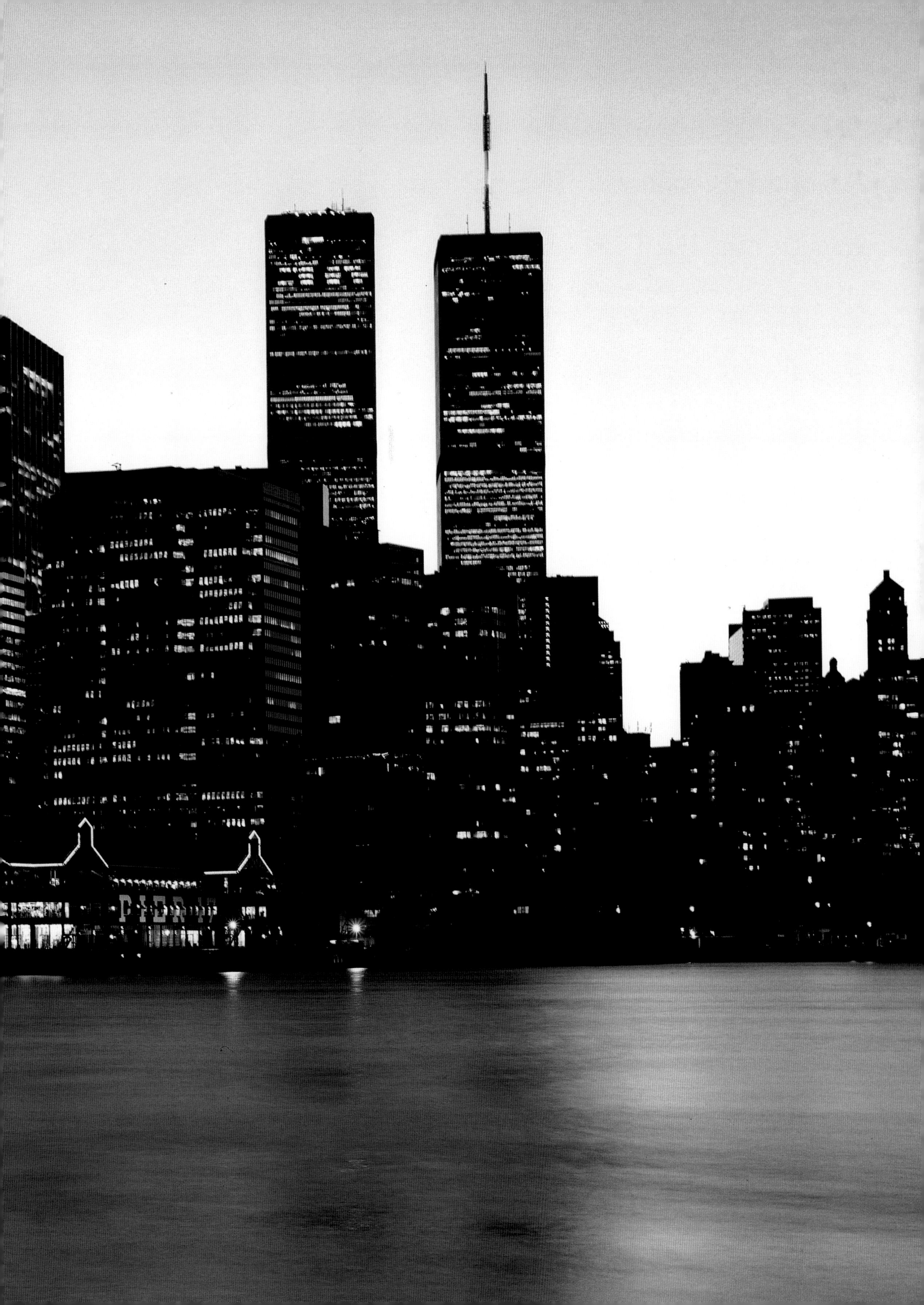

The South Street Seaport Museum (left and above) was a creation of the Rouse Company in cooperation with the city's Public Development Corporation. Whole blocks off Fulton Street were converted into a "festival marketplace" shopping and dining complex that retains vestiges of the waterfront wharves and fish market. The Smithsonian Institution's National Museum of the American Indian (overleaf) is located in the 1907 United States Custom House, one of New York's grandest Beaux Arts buildings. It dates from the period before income taxes when customs duties were the nation's principal source of revenue. The U.S. Customs Service moved operations to the World Trade Center in 1973.

Trinity Church (right) at Broadway and Wall Street, designed by Richard Upjohn, rose in 1846. Its three massive bronze doors were created by Richard Morris Hunt. They recall Ghiberti's doors on the Baptistry in Florence. The AIA Guide to New York called the structure an "anthracite jewel," so dark was its color, but a 1991 restoration of the sandstone revealed the church's color is pink. New Yorkers Alexander Hamilton, the nation's first treasury secretary, and Robert Fulton, inventor of the steamboat, are among the notables buried in the Trinity Church graveyard (opposite) in the city's Wall Street section. The spire of the church itself was the tallest structure in town, visible for miles on Manhattan and from Brooklyn and Queens, until the first skyscraper was built in 1887.

Trowbridge & Livingston's neo-classical pediment was added to the 1903 New York Stock Exchange Building (opposite) in 1923. The stone of the allegorical figures deteriorated so badly that the exchange replaced them with sheet metal figures—secretly, for it did not want the public to regard any part of the operation as vulnerable. The building has a public entrance and viewing gallery. George Washington took his first oath of office on a balcony of Federal Hall (left)—not this building in Lower Manhattan but the old City Hall, called Federal Hall, on this site. The current imposing Greek Revival structure, now a national memorial, was built in 1842 as a custom house.

Arturo DiModica's three-and-a-half-ton bronze Charging Bull (above), sculpted in response to the stock market slump of 1987, has become a symbol of New York's Wall Street. The New York Stock Exchange floor (opposite) is a nonstop, and now high-tech, beehive of activity. About two hundred million shares of stock are traded each day here, now more often by computer than by shouts from frenzied brokers. OVERLEAF: From the East River, the twin 110-story towers of the World Trade Center—just two of five office buildings in the complex—hover over the rest of Lower Manhattan. The elevator in Two World Trade Center takes just fifty-eight seconds to reach the 107th-floor observation deck. Another in One World Trade Center is just as speedy to the Windows on the World restaurant.

Cass Gilbert's older, more ornate Ninety West Street Building stands in marked contrast to the World Trade Center towers (above). The smaller limestone-and-terra-cotta office building was erected in 1907. OPPOSITE: More than twenty workers died building the Brooklyn Bridge, the world's first steel suspension bridge—including its German-born designer, engineer John Roebling. Many laborers suffered attacks of the bends working in the under-water caissons that became footings for the bridge's towers. Each weekday morning and afternoon, there's a rush-hour scramble on the bridge, not only involving automobiles but also among the thousands of pedes-trians and bicyclists heading to work and home across its span. Built from 1867 to 1883, the bridge helped spur the development of "Greater New York" that swallowed Brooklyn and three other new "boroughs" into the expanded New York City.

The cast-iron Haughwout Building (left) on lower Broadway was designed by James Gaynor and erected in 1857 to house Eder Haughwout's glass, china, and silverware emporium. It was here that Elisha Graves Otis installed the first commercial "safety" passenger elevator in the country. OPPOSITE: The names of the city's five boroughs are etched into the pediment of the 1909 Police Headquarters Building on Centre Street. ("Richmond" was the original name for Staten Island County.) Despite the building's presence, contraband whiskey flowed so freely during Prohibition that nearby Grand Street was called "Bootleggers' Row." The police moved out of the building in 1973, and in 1985 it was converted into luxury co-op apartments, some of which were purchased by international sports, fashion, and entertainment personalities.

Galleries, clothing and curio shops, grocery stores, and restaurants abound in Chinatown (right), which has expanded from three to more than forty square blocks. Its more than 150,000 residents make New York's Chinatown not only larger than San Francisco's, but also the largest Chinese community outside of Asia. Tortuously narrow and crooked streets are especially crowded around Chinese New Year in mid-winter. There's a Chinatown History Museum at the corner of Bayard and Mulberry streets whose collections highlight Asian Americans' labor history. But Chinese restaurants are by no means confined to Chinatown. China Fun (above) on Columbus Avenue, for one, introduced several "fusion" dishes combined from different cultures, including seafood papillote and various kinds of barbecued meats.

The size of Little Italy (above) has shrunk as Chinatown expands. Savory holdouts, including restaurants, cheese shops, and delicatessens, can be found along Mulberry Street. Little Italy's first residents—immigrant laborers and their families from the southern Italian peninsula—were crammed together in "dumbbell apartments" covering seventeen square blocks. These tenements were built so close together that sunlight could not even reach their courtyards. SoHo's Greene Street (opposite) is a warren of antique shops, studios, and loft apartments in converted tenement buildings. The district includes the largest surviving concentration of cast-iron-fronted architecture in the world. Saving many of these buildings from demolition in the path of a proposed Lower Manhattan Expressway was one of preservationists' greatest achievements. Fire escapes were too often an afterthought: so numerous were the conflagrations in warehouses filled with flammables that the neighborhood was called "Hell's Hundred Acres."

Artsy SoHo is filled
with galleries such as
Mimi Ferzt's (right),
where M. Chemiakin's
1993 bronze Cybele:
Goddess of Fertility
is a prominent fixture.
ABOVE: Many lofts
are sold as commercial
space, where an
almost unimaginable
variety of small busi-
nesses, artists, and
writers operate.
Because many of
SoHo's buildings were
once warehouses with
high ceilings, even
large paintings and
sculptures can be
worked on and sold
from these spaces.
But rising prices
have driven many
artists to other neigh-
borhoods. The name
SoHo was coined
not only to designate
its location south of
Houston (pronounced
HOW-stun) Street,
but also to affect the
ambience of London's
gritty Soho District.

MI FERZT GALLERY

Washington Square (left) grew up on a former potter's field and parade ground. Stanford White executed its magnificent marble arch in 1895 to replace a wooden arch that had marked the centennial of George Washington's first inauguration downtown. Many former mansions on "The Row" across the street have been taken over by New York University. ABOVE: A homeless artist created the impromptu sculpture in front of the offices of the Village Voice, which publishes a comprehensive list of events in TriBeCa, SoHo, and Greenwich Village. OVERLEAF: In Greenwich Village, rents that were once cheap attracted writers like Walt Whitman and Edgar Allan Poe, and artists like Albert Bierstadt and John La Farge.

Artwork in the Village is not confined to galleries and studio lofts. Murals like Clayton Patterson's creation (above) on Avenue A are part of the eclectic street scene in the East Village. RIGHT: Even tiny firehouses like the one in Greenwich Village blend into the diverse milieu. OVERLEAF: Viewed from the Queens shore, the Midtown Manhattan skyline shows some breaks in the skyscrapers. The United Nations Secretariat is at the left, the Chrysler Building's lighted, stainless-steel tower splits the frame, and other U.N. buildings appear along the waterfront. The structure below and to the left of the main United Nations Building is Tudor City, a mock-Tudor complex of more than three thousand apartments built in the 1920s.

New York Governor Samuel Tilden so feared his opponents in the Tweed Ring that he had rolling steel doors built into his Gramercy Park home. The building, with its lovely stonework detail (above), now houses the National Arts Club. RIGHT: Chicago architect Daniel Burnham's 1902 Fuller Building overlooking Madison Square drew gasps of astonishment from New Yorkers.

The elaborate, limestone-clad structure—later renamed the Flatiron Building because of its wedge shape—is only six feet wide at its apex. OPPOSITE: The National Park Service operates Theodore Roosevelt's birthplace on East Twentieth Street. The original house was destroyed but later faithfully reconstructed by Theodate Pope Riddle as a memorial to the energetic president.

Haunted houses are commonplace across America, but not haunted restaurants. Looking at the condition of the "doormen," one has to wonder about the Jekyll and Hyde Club "for Eccentric Explorers and Mad Scientists" (above) on Seventh Avenue. RIGHT: Carnegie Hall was built in 1891, when Pyotr Ilich Tchaikovsky conducted the New York Philharmonic's opening concert. The hall's acoustics are legendary, though some purists argue that they will never match the pristine sound prior to extensive renovation for its centennial. A museum was added, chronicling the auditorium's illustrious performances, not only by classical-music geniuses but also by popular musicians like Count Basie and Benny Goodman.

When the white marble and stone Saint Patrick's Cathedral (opposite) was built in the late 1870s and named for the patron saint of Ireland, parishioners scoffed at the location, far up Fifth Avenue at Fiftieth Street, out in the "country." Many wanted to put a graveyard on the site instead, but Archbishop John Hughes prevailed and bought land from the city for $83. Architect James Renwick Jr.'s French Gothic creation would soon be regarded as New York's finest Gothic structure. Its twin spires rise 330 feet across from Rockefeller Center. RIGHT: The 1872 Moorish-style Central Synagogue on Lexington Avenue is the oldest continually used Jewish synagogue in the city. It was designed by Henry Fernbach, the nation's first prominent Jewish architect.

58

SAINT
JOSEPH

PATRON OF
THE CHURCH

SAINT
PATRICK

PATRON OF
THIS CHURCH

ST. ISAAC JOGUES
MARTYR

FIRST PRIEST
IN NEW YORK

ST. FRANCES X.
CABRINI

MOTHER OF
THE IMMIGRANT

VEN. KATERI
TEKAKWITHA

LILY OF
THE MOHAWKS

MOTHER ELIZA-
BETH SETON

DAUGHTER OF
NEW YORK

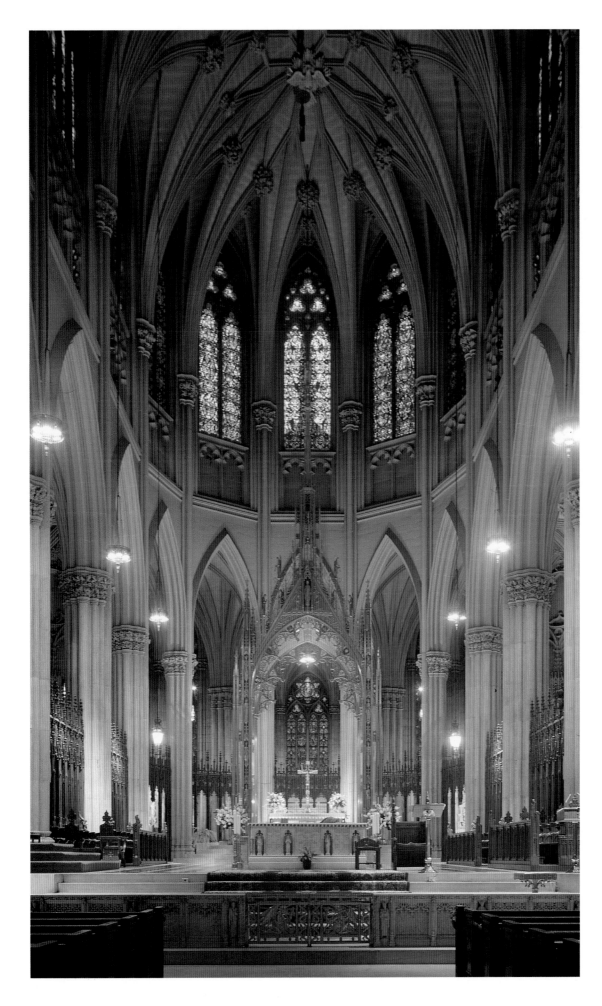

The great baldachin, or canopy, above Saint Patrick's Cathedral's high altar (left) is made of bronze. Artisans in Chartres and Nantes crafted most of the cathedral's stained-glass windows. Architect James Renwick Jr.— an Episcopalian— was only thirty-two when he accepted the commission to build the great cathedral, which took twenty-one years, beginning in 1858, to complete. His effort upstaged Richard Upjohn's work on Trinity Church downtown. But architectural critics fussed (and still do) that Renwick's work was incomplete: its Gothic edifice has the requisite spires but not flying buttresses. The Lady Chapel, behind the altar, was added in 1906 by Charles T. Mathews. Saint Patrick's great bronze doors (opposite) weigh twenty thousand pounds; their statues depict some of New York's saints.

Henry Hardenbergh, who had designed the Dakota apartment building and the Waldorf-Astoria Hotel, designed the French Renaissance–style Plaza Hotel (opposite). It included extensive apartments for the Rockefellers and other prominent New York families. Fifth Avenue (above) has become synonymous with wealth and high society. As high-end jewelry and department stores gradually moved up the avenue, they displaced—or moved into—some of the city's finest mansions. An aggressive merchants' association helped to sustain the elegance of Fifth Avenue by keeping out billboards, parking lots, and street vendors. No "els" clattered by, either; instead there were an independent Fifth Avenue Transportation Company's horse-drawn omnibuses, followed later by open-top double-deck buses. Though only four of the latter existed, they were fondly remembered when they disappeared, especially since the grand ride up the avenue cost no more than a subway ride.

Macy's (left), the
world's largest depart-
ment store, was
founded by a former
whaler. It covers a full
city block down West
Thirty-fourth Street
from the Empire State
Building. Fashion
trends for much of the
nation are set in the
city's Garment
District, now called
the Fashion Center.
The series of produc-
tion warehouses,
showrooms, and
workshops has been
pinpointed by a street
statue of a garment
worker (above) on
Seventh Avenue.
New York's "rag trade"
employed East
European Jews, then
gradually Asians,
Hispanics, and other
immigrants, some-
times in deplorable
sweatshops, first on
the Lower East Side,
then in the Thirties
on the West Side.
Faced with increasing
international compe-
tition, responsible
industry leaders have
worked to expose and
correct such conditions
as well as clean up
and better patrol the
neighborhood.

New York Mayor Fiorello La Guardia named E. C. Potter's two lions at the New York Public Library's main building on Bryant Park (above) "Patience" and "Fortitude." The AIA Guide to New York City calls Carrère and Hastings's 1911 building "the apogee of Beaux Arts for New York." The library's Jefferson Market branch (opposite) on lower Avenue of the Americas was a combination courthouse, jail, and produce market designed by Calvert Vaux and Frederick Clark Withers, completed in 1874, and once voted one of the ten most beautiful buildings in America by a poll of the nation's architects. Especially notable is the building's beautiful brick-arched basement—now the library's reference room—which was used as a passageway for prisoners on their way to jail or trial. The building has a firewatchers' balcony, and the bell that summoned volunteer firefighters still hangs in the tower.

Bryant Park, in the shadow of the main city library building on East Forty-second street, had deteriorated into an open-air drug market in the 1960s and '70s. But a community-business partnership, the Bryant Park Restoration Corporation, turned the park into a safe, inviting place. The Bryant Park Grill (left), ample park benches (above), and a spacious green beckon visitors. Films are shown at the park on summer evenings, and there are fashion shows and concerts as well. In the 1850s, Bryant Park, which adjoined the Croton Distributing Reservoir that supplied New Yorkers with fresh water, housed a sparkling Crystal Palace, built for the World's Fair of 1853.

Jules-Alexis Coutans's sculpture of Mercury, Hercules, and Minerva crowns the main entrance of the 1913 Grand Central Terminal (right), which blocks Park Avenue. The commuter station was meticulously restored in the early 1990s. The New York Life Insurance Company's building on Madison Avenue (above), designed in 1928 by Cass Gilbert, was built on the site of the first Madison Square Garden. Only after train lines were buried did Park Avenue (overleaf) attain its status as the city's boulevard of posh hotels, private palaces, and apartment buildings—perhaps the world's priciest strip of real estate. Several expensive office towers have been added to the avenue.

D CENTRAL
RMINAL

New York's theater district is legendary. Times Square (above)—which is actually triangular— is a neon wonderland that turns raucous on New Year's Eve. It was long known as the "Crossroads of the World," in deference to the New York Times, *which later moved to new headquarters not far away. The Shubert Theatre (right) on West Forty-* fourth was named for impresario Sam S. Shubert. Actors lined up along "Shubert Alley," hoping for parts in a Shubert play. The musical A Chorus Line *ran for a record 6,137 performances at the Shubert. Television personalities still keep late hours in and around the Ed Sullivan Theater (overleaf) on Broadway.*

In its lobby, the Empire State Building (right) salutes itself as the "Eighth Wonder of the World." The building (above) included a tower designed— but never used— to moor zeppelins. Its 102nd-floor observatory became a hot tourist destination. William Van Alen's seventy-seven-story Art Deco Chrysler Building (opposite), clad in stainless steel, combined practical engineering and stunning decoration and it typified the race to be the world's tallest building: its shining spire was hidden in the fire shaft until the unveiling, then dramatically raised to give it supremacy over a bank building downtown. But it was the world's tallest for only a few months, until the Empire State Building opened. The Chrysler Building's fluorescent lancet crown glimmers over the New York skyline at night.

Begun during the
Great Depression of
the 1930s, Rockefeller
Center became the
city's "second down-
town." It combines
nineteen entertain-
ment, shopping, and
office buildings, with
the towering General
Electric Building
(above) at its hub.
Underground passage-
ways connect the
center's restaurants,
network television
studios, doctors'
offices, boutiques,
banks, and publishers'
headquarters. The rink
at Rockefeller Center
(right) is a popular
cold-weather attrac-
tion. It gives way to
an outdoor restaurant
in warmer months
and is towered over
by a huge Christmas
tree each Yuletide.
Paul Manship created
the Prometheus
statue in 1934.

Fodor's *guide calls the intersection of Fifth Avenue and Fifty-seventh Street "ground zero for high-class shopping." The renowned jeweler Tiffany & Co.— famous for its alluring window displays (right)—anchors that location. In the movie* Breakfast at Tiffany's, *Audrey Hepburn window-shopped there. Radio City Music Hall (opposite), part of Rockefeller Center, hosts musical spectaculars, big-name concerts, and the high-stepping Rockettes' Christmas and Easter specials. When it opened in 1932 as a variety house, it was the world's largest theater, including a 110-foot stage in several levels and a fifty-foot turntable. Radio City soon became primarily a movie house with occasional stage extravaganzas. Next door is "Diamond Row," born when Jewish diamond merchants in Antwerp and Amsterdam fled Nazism in the late 1930s.*

The United Nations complex (opposite) was designed by an international committee, led by American Wallace Harrison. It sits on land that once supported Turtle Bay farms, then squalid tenement houses. Today it is technically international territory—there is even an American Embassy on the property! The familiar glass-walled tower houses neither the General Assembly nor the Security Council; it is the Secretariat Building, in which bureaucrats of many nations labor. Tours are conducted in several languages. The brick and glass Ford Foundation Building (above), designed by Kevin Roche, John Dinkeloo & Associates in 1967, includes an elaborate indoor garden. New York's West Side skyline (overleaf) shows just how prominent grand apartment buildings became in the city's life. Gentrification has come to the commercial streets— upper Broadway, Amsterdam Avenue, and Columbus Avenue—making the blocks of apartment buildings an even more desirable address.

The Dakota (left and above) on Central Park West, the first grand apartment on Manhattan's Upper West Side, was truly "out west" in wide-open spaces when it opened in 1880. It was built in the 1880s for Edward Clark, heir to the Singer sewing machine fortune, and dubbed "Clark's Folly" for its location, so far from city grandeur. Curiosity still compels tourists to peek past the doorman of the building where John Lennon lived and outside of which he was murdered by a deranged fan in 1980. The luxury apartment building has been the address of a long list of other stars as well.

Elevated transit—
the "el"—opened
the Upper West Side
(left and opposite) to
development, begin-
ning in the 1870s.
Once the Dakota
appeared in the 1880s,
a rush of construction
of other luxury apart-
ments and hotels
followed. Some were
brownstone, others
intricately orna-
mented brick and
limestone. Less sleek
than the Upper East
Side—and downright
shabby in spots during
the 1970s and 1980s—
a reinvigorated
Upper West Side
became a reasonably
affordable neighbor-
hood of professionals.
OVERLEAF: A pro-
cession of famous
architects, from
Calvert Vaux to John
Russell Pope, had
a hand in the design
and expansions
of the Romanesque
Revival American
Museum of Natural
History. The world's
most extensive
collection of fossil
vertebrates, and
minerals, gems,
and meteor frag-
ments, are among its
millions of artifacts.

American Museum of Natural History

Once a tawdry street lined with tenements, Columbus Avenue on the Upper West Side was rehabilitated and renovated (as well as razed in some blocks) and has become a lively boulevard of boutiques, restaurants (above), and clubs. The restaurants run the gamut of international cuisine; several feature imaginative decor, extensive wine lists, and expensive prices. One of its most unusual retail establishments is Maxilla & Mandible, a natural-history store that sells skeletons, shells, antlers, and even butterflies. (A maxilla is a jaw, especially a mammal's upper jaw; a mandible is a lower jaw.) Other stores on Columbus Avenue sell eccentric windup toys, giant crayons, and bizarre stationery. OVERLEAF: Central Park West has its own historic district between West Seventy-fifth and West Seventy-seventh streets. It includes several Gothic and neo-Grecian row houses and apartment buildings that predate the twentieth century.

MAXILLA & MANDIBLE'S
CARCHARODON MEGALODON

Frederick Law Olmsted and Calvert Vaux turned wretched bogs, pig farms, and squatters' shacks into beautiful Central Park—New York's "backyard," forever protected from development. The bronze statue in the reflecting pool of the Conservatory Garden (opposite) is of Mary and Dickon from Frances Hodgson Burnett's The Secret Garden. *Originally cast in 1932, Paul Manship's bronze* Group of Bears *(top left) stands near the Friedman Playground. A favorite stop for brunch or dinner is the Tavern on the Green (bottom), which got a rare commercial spot in Central Park thanks to the pull of one of its first owners—Tammany Hall's "Boss" Tweed.* Overleaf: *The Bethesda Terrace is the only formal architectural element in Olmsted and Vaux's original plan. The centerpiece fountain features a bronze, winged* Angel of the Waters.

Upper East Side brownstones (opposite and top left) are among the city's most coveted apartment buildings. This moneyed enclave represents the "high life" that is associated with New York society. A fortunate few live in units covered by rent control; others pay astronomical sums each month for the apartments' convenience, comfort, and prestige. This area has a historic district, but most New Yorkers refer to the area of museums, chanceries, and apartment palaces between Fifth and Lexington avenues on the Upper East Side as simply the "Gold Coast." Bistros such as Trois Jean (bottom) on East Seventy-ninth Street capture New Yorkers' taste for home-style— yet exotic—food. The restaurant was named for its chef, pastry chef, and manager, who shared the same first name.

Shipping magnate Archibald Gracie built a handsome home (top right) on the East River in 1799. A century later, the city appropriated the mansion and made it a museum. It became the mayoral residence during Fiorello La Guardia's administration.
BOTTOM: *Just as he coordinated work on the United Nations complex, Wallace Harrison supervised several architects on the cluster of perform-ing-arts institutions called Lincoln Center.*
OPPOSITE: *Sotheby's auction house handles all kinds of fine and decorative arts, including masterwork paintings like this seventeenth-century Michael Sweerts work* A Plague in an Ancient City *and this French Royal Silver tureen offered at $7.5 million.*
OVERLEAF: *The collection of the Metropolitan Museum of Art — the largest museum in the Western Hemi-sphere—includes galleries of arms, armor, and heraldry.*

Roman emperor Augustus's three-room Temple of Dendur (above), completed in 15 B.C., is now a featured exhibit of the Metropolitan Museum of Art. The museum was founded in 1870 by a group of wealthy philanthropists who envisioned a great museum to rival those in Europe. Every continent is represented in its collections, and some of the world's greatest traveling exhibitions visit as well. The museum's prized holdings include the portrait of Gertrude Stein by Pablo Picasso, Emanuel Gottlieb Leutze's Washington Crossing the Delaware, one of Rembrandt's self-portraits, Vincent Van Gogh's Cypresses, tiny models depicting daily life at the time of ancient Egyptian nobleman Mekutra, and a forty-five-thousand-piece collection of costumes from the seventeenth century to today. New York streets are also replete with art. The 1993 sculpture Yahkin by Boaz Vaadia (opposite) stands outside the Ninety-sixth Street Association offices.

The Jewish Museum (left) uptown on Fifth Avenue holds America's largest collection of Judaica—including Torah headpieces, circumcision instruments, and reminders of the Holocaust. The core 1908 French Renaissance building was originally the home of financier Felix Warburg. The Reform Jewish Congregation Emanu-El—"God is with us"—was formed in 1845. Over the years, the congregation moved uptown, finally settling into one of the largest synagogues in the world (detail above) on East Sixty-fifth at Fifth Avenue. Known throughout the city as simply "The Temple," the building was completed in 1929 following Emanu-El's merger with the Beth-El congregation.

The best way to tour the collection of modern and contemporary art in Frank Lloyd Wright's Guggenheim Museum (opposite) is from the top down, via a spiraling ramp.

Wright received the commission for his only New York building in 1942; it was not completed until a few months after his death in 1959. In 1992, the museum—named for Solomon R. Guggenheim, a collector of avant-garde art—added a downtown site in SoHo. The museum features works by Chagall, Picasso, Kandinsky, and others.

ABOVE: New York City's religious diversity is underlined by the gray-granite Islamic Center of New York, built in 1991. The mosque serves the city's 400,000 Muslims as well as diplomats and visitors from Muslim nations. Architects Skidmore, Owings & Merrill used a computer to be certain the building faced Mecca, as required by Islamic law.

John Duncan's memorial to Union general Ulysses Grant (above), popularly known as "Grant's Tomb," is modeled after Napoleon's tomb and other memorials. Bronze busts in the crypt, sculpted during the Great Depression, depict Grant's greatest subordinates.

OPPOSITE: Daniel Chester French's Alma Mater, which was completed in 1903 at the entrance to Columbia University's library, survived a bomb blast during violent student demonstrations in 1968. The campus, which is well concealed behind fences along upper Broadway and Amsterdam Avenue, is ringed by coffeehouses and cafés.

OVERLEAF: More than ten thousand worshipers can gather at once at the Cathedral of St. John the Divine on Amsterdam Avenue. The neo-Gothic building has been under construction for more than a century. Its exterior statues are the creations of the Stoneworks program, begun in 1978 for English stonemasons to teach American workers their demanding trade.

The Divine Peace Fountain (opposite) was constructed in the small park next to the Cathedral of St. John the Divine along Amsterdam Avenue to celebrate the two-hundredth anniversary of the Episcopal Diocese of New York. The figures represent the triumph of good over evil as well as representations of other opposing forces: violence and harmony, light and darkness, life and death. The fountain is surrounded by tiny cast-bronze children's sculptures, chosen in periodic competitions. ABOVE: Also near Columbia University stands the old Audubon Theatre Building, once a 2,368-seat movie palace. Its extravagant terra-cotta-glazed polychromy face was designed in 1912 by Thomas W. Lamb. In the building's giant ballroom, Black Muslim leader Malcolm X was assassinated at a rally in 1965. The building has been extensively renovated for commercial use.

LEFT: *Inside the Metropolitan Museum of Art's medieval-style Cloisters in Fort Tryon Park, a fifteenth-century Spanish tempera and oil triptych hangs above a German altarpiece, c. 1470, and busts of female saints. In another room hangs* The Lamentation (above), *a walnut, polychromy, and gilded piece, c. 1450–1500, that was originally the centerpiece of a large altar flanked by painted wings. An extensive tapestry collection and an arcaded courtyard are other highlights of these cloisters, some of which were imported from France and Spain and reassembled here.* OVERLEAF: *A magnificent stained-glass window inspires parishioners at the 1923 Abyssinian Baptist Church on West 138th Street in Harlem.*

The Cotton Club nightclub (opposite) moved in 1978 from its original location to a spot under the entryway to the George Washington Bridge. The club still features blues and jazz on "Harlem's Main Street." Sylvan Terrace's 1882 row houses (left) are one of Upper Manhattan's finest addresses. They present "a revived memory of very old New York," according to the AIA Guide to New York City. Just across the street in a park stands the Morris-Jumel Mansion, built by Roger Morris as a summer residence. The mansion was George Washington's headquarters early in the Revolutionary War, but his forces were ousted from the home—and all of Manhattan— by the British. It became, among other things, a tavern before being pur- chased by a wealthy French merchant, Stephen Jumel.

Convent Avenue (above) in Hamilton Heights is lined with townhouses. Named for the first U.S. secretary of the treasury, Alexander Hamilton, who built a country estate there, Hamilton Heights was developed after the West Side elevated railway made its way to far-north Manhattan. Hamilton called his home "the Grange." Archenemy Aaron Burr was living in the nearby Morris-Jumel Mansion when he killed Hamilton in a duel in 1804. Hamilton Heights once included the New England–style village of Manhattan-ville, where pigment was manufactured, yarn was milled, Yuengling Beer was brewed, and Manhat-tan College was founded (it later moved to Riverdale). Sylvia's soul-food emporium (opposite), a Harlem institution, features southern breakfasts and a Sunday gospel brunch and dinner. Its newsletter describes Sylvia and Herbert Woods's restaurant as being "of Harlem and the world."

Index

Playground basketball is an art form at Public School 101 on Lexington Avenue in East, or "Spanish,"

Harlem. Always a working-class neighborhood, it was once known as "Italian Harlem."